Daddy, Don't! Mommy, Why?

A story of childhood sexual abuse

by

Jacqueline Aaron

Daddy, Don'! Mommy, Why? © *2012.*
All rights reserved by Argus Enterprises International, Inc.

No part of this book may be reproduced or transmitted in any form or by any means, graphic, electronic, or mechanical, including photocopying, recording, taping, or by any informational storage retrieval system without prior permission in writing from the publisher.

Black Nite Publishers

For information:
Argus Enterprises International, Inc.
9001 Ridge Hill Street
Kernersville, North Carolina 27285
www.a-argusbooks.com

ISBN: 978-0-6157699-9-2
ISBN: 0-6157699-9-9-7

Book Cover designed by Dubya

Printed in the United States of America

Introduction

I don't claim to be much of an author; in fact, this is my first attempt at writing a full-length book. I have had experience in the past writing newsletters for our ladies clubs and garden clubs. I have had several letters published by various newspapers as I am an outspoken activist and not afraid to express my opinion on virtually any subject. Still, I would never have given the concept of a book a thought except for the fact that three women came to see me. Shirley Jean—she asked that I don't use her full name as many of her friends are not aware of her circumstances—had been receiving treatment from my cousin Carolyn who is a psychiatrist in Charlotte. Carolyn had suggested that the women should talk to me as she was aware that I was a bull-headed full charger when it was a cause that I believed in. And I had gotten enough information from Shirley Jean when she called me to realize that this was definitely a cause that I could believe in. Child abuse is undoubtedly the most evil thing that a human being can perpetrate on another and to make that child a sexual victim is even more contemptible. Still, nothing in the telephone conversation with Shirley Jean had prepared me for the stories that I would soon be hearing from three of the bravest people that I had ever known.

Statistics tells us that one of every six females suffer sexual molestation before they reach the age of eighteen. If you think that is bad, be advised that according to government surveys, most cases of sexual molestation are not reported and thus are not part of the statistics. That would mean that the incidents of sexual molestation is far greater than one in six and may well be half of the females are molested. As to the reason that most cases are not reported, sources reveal that the majority of all cases are perpetrated by a member of the family or a close friend of the family. It is not unusual to learn of a case where a father, a son or a step-father has molested a young girl, and if it is true that most cases are not reported, just think of the poor females who have suffered.

The three women arrived at my house in Raleigh early in the morning. Joining me in taking a cup of coffee, we made small talk, trying to get comfortable with each other. Finally, Shirley Jean blurted it out. "Ms. Aaron – Jacqueline – we want you to write a book about our stories."

Having been somewhat pre-warned by our earlier telephone conversation, I was none the less hesitant to agree. I told the women about the limited experience that I had with the written word, but that didn't seem to faze them. They – by now, all three were talking – commented that I had been highly recommended as someone who would get personally involved and they wanted me to be the person to tell the world about their experiences. It took them a long while before they could persuade me and the closing argument – the one that got me all charged up – was the information that their sexual molester was their own father. That did it.

Over the next several hours, I recorded their stories on my mini recorder so that I wouldn't miss any of the trauma, the pain and suffering that these women had been subjected to while they were still just children, virtually infants. When I began with the book, I listened to those stories over and over, crying unabashedly every time that I listened, just as I had when they were revealing their tragedy the first day. Only now some of the tears were not tears of sympathy, rather these were hot tears of anger. Anger at a society that would allow a monster such as this to survive, a society that would allow a mother like this to subject her children to such anguish. Anger at all mankind, and I wouldn't have cared a bit if God decided at that moment that man was too evil to exist and destroyed the world with a blast of righteousness wrath.

As I started working on this manuscript I suggested to the three women that we should use a self-publisher and make just three copies, one for each of them. I told them that in that way none of their friends or acquaintances would learn of their history. That suggestion was met with immediate disapproval. "We want the world to know. We want everyone to know that children are not safe, are being abused every day, are sexual victims of depraved monsters, even in their own families." To these angry women, this was the primary purpose of writing a book, even if it was a book that didn't sell well.

"In addition," Shirley Jean added, "we want women out there everywhere to understand that they are not alone in what they have suffered. We know that most of them were either sexually molested or at least sexually harassed, and we want them to know that we understand. We want to offer ourselves as proof that you can overcome the molestation, after all, it isn't your fault, you were the victim."

After that comment, all I could do was agree to undertake this task. And believe you me—with the revelations of just how evil and depraved man can be—just putting these words down on paper is a task, and not a welcomed task. Still, I gave my word that I would do my best and that I would remain faithful to the chore. In doing so, I have not tried to soft-peddle their words, and in fact, have tried to use their precise words. In doing so, perhaps the grammar and the phrasing may not be as precise and neat as it could be, but these stories are not precise or neat, they are tales of anguish and suffering, the like of which should never be visited on anyone, especially children.

So, on behalf of Shirley Jean, Martha Sue and Patricia Ann, I offer their experiences so that sexual victims everywhere—female and male, as I have since learned—so that they can take heart in the fact that what happened to them does not degrade them in any fashion, rather the acts stand as an indictment of the perpetrators, and some day they will face justice, if not here in this world, then when they finally face God himself. Then justice will be served.

Shirley Jean

You'll just have to excuse me if I am just a bit uncomfortable. I'll try not to stutter and won't blubber—at least not too much. This is really the first time that I have ever told anybody about my life except for my therapist and I'm not exactly sure how what I am saying will come out, but I promised both my sisters that if they would tell the truth, then so would I, no matter how hard it is to talk about and no matter if anyone believes me or not. I know that Martha Sue—we called her Martha—and Patricia Ann—or Patty—will know the truth when they hear it; after all, they had to live through it as well as I did. I also will not promise that my writing is perfect or that my grammar or spelling is one hundred percent accurate because my grades weren't that high in school and as you read this, you may understand why. Anyway, I will do the best I can and ask that anybody reading this understand the emotional stress that I am in as I put these words down on paper.

I am finally telling all of this because my therapist felt that it would be a relief and he lp me improve, if I could talk about it. That's easy for a psychiatrist to say, but it's much harder when it is your life and your situation. I agreed to do so only after my therapist talked with me and my sisters all together, and both Martha Sue and Patricia Ann agreed that if I would, they would. Having learned about my circumstances for th e first time during that joint session, it wasn't long before the therapist had us all sobbing and blubbering as we each tried to talk about our childhood. It was the hardest thing I have ever had to endure in my lifetime. To realize what my depraved father did to my young sisters hurt me even more than my father hurt me with his devilish actions and abuse.

To begin with, my – or our – home life wasn't anything that you would want anyone to go through; certainly not a child. True, there are other poor people out there in the world, even today, but we were more than poor, we were destitute. Although my father was there when I was quite small, my recollection of him at that time is vague. I really didn't know much about my father before he went off to war. From what I can remember about what my mother told me, he was a kind and gentle person, friendly and giving. I remember him coming home, though; it was about a month before my fifth birthday. I remember because that was going to be my birthday present. That was really about all that we could afford. While he was gone, things were very tough for our family. There was my mother and my two sisters, Martha—who was one year younger than me—and Patricia, who was two years younger than me. We didn't have any money and my mother had to work as a waitress at one of the restaurants—which I found out after I grew up a little was actually a bar/adult club—just to have enough money to buy food and pay the rent. We lived in a small apartment, just a living room/kitchen/dining room combination and two bedrooms. My two sisters and I slept in one of the bedrooms, but I did have a bed by myself while Martha and Patricia—Patty—slept together in another bed. Sometimes at night I could hear noises coming from my mother's room; it sounded like she was crying or something. I didn't know what because she had forbidden me to ever open her door, even if she wasn't home. Of course, at the time, I believed that adults never cried, after all, they were grown-ups. There were also times that I believed that I heard two voices in the room, but I can't say for sure because my mother insisted that I be in bed before she came home. I do know that there were other noises coming out of her room, sounded like she was bouncing around on the bed. She would sleep late every morning and wouldn't even get out of bed until we kids had finished our lunch. Then she would make us go to our room and stay there until she called us to come back out. There were a whole bunch of times that you could hear someone going down the steps, but after a while, she would call us back into the kitchen area where we would sit at the little table and she would listen as I would try to teach my sisters the alphabet and how to count.

Of course, now as an adult, I have a much better understanding as to what was going on, but at the time I was only five years old and no one had ever taught me about sex or anything like that.

Even now I can recall the hunger pangs that I often felt when there wasn't enough food for us all. We would eat oatmeal in the morning, oatmeal at lunch and oatmeal for supper. Sometimes we had enough milk to mix with the oatmeal, but most of the time my mother just cooked it with water, saving what little milk we had for my youngest sister. For a change of pace, sometimes grits were on sale and my mother would buy enough for a week or two, otherwise it was oatmeal. Ugh. Once in a while, my mother would bring home some raisins from her job, or maybe sandwich or two, when she could get one. Most of the time, she ate where she worked and that left the oatmeal for the three of us. She would put us to bed early, around five o'clock, I believe, and then she would go to work, getting home sometimes in the night. Sometimes in the night I would wake up and miss her, and sometimes I would have to hold either Patty or Martha—or both—as they cried from being scared. As the oldest child, I felt that I needed to take care of my sisters while our mother would be at work. Does the words, 'home alone' mean anything to you. Can you imagine a child less than five years old being left in charge of a three-year-old and a two-year-old without supervision? I suppose that we were fortunate in that nothing happened to us while our mother was at work.

You will notice that I always refer to my mother as 'my mother' or as 'Mother' and never as 'Mom' or 'Mommy'. By the time I finish talking, you will understand why I can't, and you will also know why I can never refer to my father as Dad or Daddy or Pop. Just to think about it gives me the shivers.

I was happy that I would soon be five years old. You had to be five in order to go to the pre-school program in our town. There was kindergarten and day-care of course, but those cost money and our mother told us that we didn't have any money for foolish things like that. In fact, we never seemed to have money for anything. For our birthdays, we were lucky to have even a small cake, and for Christmas there were people from the nearby church who would bring us bags of fruit, some candy and perhaps a few clothes, most of which were second hand. Mother would rant and raise hell about that, slinging the clothes across the floor. But then I would have to pick up the items she threw just so we kids could have something to wear. Of course, we never went to church as Mother didn't want the neighbors to see just how destitute we really were. Truth is that we didn't get much involved with religion as she wasn't really an advocate for Christianity.

While Mother worked, I had to keep the house clean, although three rooms and a bath doesn't make much of a house, in fact, it was an apartment upstairs over a furniture store. The only way to get to the apartment was by a set of iron steps attached to the outside of the building. The steps were old and rusty and groaned every time anybody tried to climb them. The best part of that was that nobody could sneak up on us but on the other hand, I would always wake up when my mother came home and climbed up those steps.

We had an old car that stayed parked in the field beside the apartment. I guess it might have run, but Mother said she didn't have any money for gas or for repairs, so she always rode to work with one of the other people who worked at the same place that she worked. Sometimes it was a man who would come and get her, but most of the time someone just blew their horn and she would take off, telling me to watch out for the other two girls. Lucky for me, both my sisters were potty-trained although it hadn't been very long since I had to change Patty's diapers and clean her when she messed. Anyway, all of us just wore the same clothes most of the time and heating up the oatmeal wasn't that big of a deal. Mother would cook enough to last us for at least a week and we did have a microwave that I could use. And to tell the truth, it's not easy to mess up oatmeal. Anyway you cut it, it isn't the most tasty food in the world.

The day before my fifth birthday, Mother was out of bed early, waking us kids and telling us to put on clean clothes. I guess that she wanted us to look our best, although our best clothes were still second-hand, having been given to us by those church people.

"Your papa's coming home today." That explained why she was up early although she had worked the night before. We didn't have a clock in the house, just the time keeper on the microwave which was never set right, so there was no way of knowing what time she had gotten home. I had heard her climb the staircase and go into her room, but then it was very quiet and I went back to sleep. Still, it didn't seem like I had slept very long, as it was hard for me to get my eyes open and get out of bed. Even the thought that my father was coming home didn't really excite me because I could barely remember him. I could remember that he had left just as Patty was being born and I know he wasn't at the hospital when she was delivered. Now, I know that he had been drafted by the Army and had to go off for training. Just having a baby was no excuse and when the Army calls you, you go. And now he was coming home. Maybe things will be a little better. Although I wasn't really excited, my mother was. At least, she seemed excited... or perhaps nervous. After all, it had been about three years since he had left.

It was just after we ate lunch that we heard someone climbing the stairway and then a knock at the door. When my mother opened the door, there was a man standing there, a man in uniform. To my surprise, I recognized him as the man who had been around when I was younger, and knew that it was my father. Although I recognized him, I was reluctant to run over and hug him, and of course, my sisters didn't know who he was. Martha had only been a year old when he left, and Patty was just being born. My mother called us, "Come over and hug your daddy." I was the only child that dared approach this strange newcomer and I just stood there beside my mother until he reached over and took me in his arms, hugging me and kissing me on my cheek. I felt a little strange as my mother had almost never hugged any of us, and his breath smelled strong, like some of the cleaner that I used on the microwave or the furniture. When he put me back on my feet and released me, I stepped back and looked up at him.

My father was a tall man, standing a little more than six feet tall, which to a five-year-old child is a little scary. I thought he was a giant. The uniform he had on was a drab brown pants, shirt, tie and jacket. He had a cap stuck in his jacket pocket and several colorful pieces of metal over his shirt pocket, which I learned were medals that he had earned in combat. He had large feet, big hands, long arms and wide shoulders. He wasn't fat at all, but wasn't really skinny either. I suppose that you could say that he was in pretty good physical condition. He had been carrying a bag, which he had laid aside as he picked me up, and now that his hands were free, he picked up the bag and followed my mother as she walked into her room.

Now that there were five of us in that little apartment, it became somewhat crowded, but things had changed somewhat. With my father at home, we were receiving a little more money, but since he was eating with us, there never seemed to be enough. Still, we were able to have meat once in a while, either some beef roast or pork roast as my father would cook the meals while my mother slept in the morning and then worked at night. She had to keep working because something called the Veterans Administration rated my father as ten percent disabled from wounds he had suffered in combat. I didn't really understand what ten percent meant nor did I know what the Veterans Administration was… it was just something that was out there that my parents were quite angry about. The wounds that my father suffered were just something else that we were allowed to talk about. My mother took us kids into our room and told us that we should never ask our father about the war or the wounds as that would upset him. So we didn't talk about where he had been or what he had done.

Even so, the additional money that my father received, small amount that it was, allowed us to move out of that apartment into a house. It was a small house on the south side of Charlotte, North Carolina and if you know anything about Charlotte then you will realize that the south side is where the poor people lived. And that was appropriate, because we were certainly poor. We still didn't have a car but we did live near a bus stop so my mother was able to ride a bus to her job and then a co-worker would drop her off after she finished her job for the night. She was still working as a hostess at the nightclub and that was to lead to trouble between my parents, but now she was coming home by herself.

The house that we moved into on South Tryon Street was a little house, but we did have three bedrooms, a dining/eating area, a kitchen and a living room. My father went to the American Legion and somehow got enough furniture to put in the living room and also got two single beds which allowed me to sleep in one of the bedrooms by myself while Patty and Martha slept in separate beds in the second bedroom. My parents shared the third bedroom, so we had enough space to move around. And we actually had closets where we could put what clothes we did have. From another place, which I now know as Veterans Helping Veterans, my father also got a whole bunch of clothes for my sisters and for me. He even got some dresses for my mother, although she didn't like to wear any of them. She didn't object to the shoes that got, at least she wore them almost all the time.

By the time we moved into the house, I was getting close to six years old. We were visited by the Social Services Department of Charlotte, who offered to enroll me in kindergarten, but my father said no, that I would be in school in less than six months, so there was no reason for me to start kindergarten, as it was too late. He did let those people enroll Martha and Patty in something like daycare or preschool. I'm not quite sure what it was, but a bus would pick my sisters up in the morning and bring them home in the afternoon. My mother didn't like that because she would often have to get out of bed early, but most of the time it was my father who helped Martha and Patty get dressed and catch the bus. My father also helped me get dressed from time to time, although I didn't need the help. In some ways it felt good to have someone to help me, but in other ways I felt just a little uneasy, as it seemed to take longer for me to get dressed with his help than it did when I dressed by myself. He always wanted to hug me, most of the time before I put on my clothes. Believing that someone finally loved me, the hugging felt good, but it also slowed down my getting dressed.

With the help of the Salvation Army, we finally got a car. The old one that had been parked at the apartment building had been left to long and the motor froze up on it, or at least that was what my father told my mother. The car that the Salvation Amy gave us did run, although the paint was blistered and rusty. It was an old brown Cadillac that someone had donated and they gave it to my father. He would use it to go to the American Legion or the Veterans of Foreign Wars clubhouses where he would spend a lot of time with other veterans, playing cards, talking and drinking. Sometimes when he came home, he would grab me and hug me, which wasn't at all nice because his breath smelled like old cleaning fluid. He would say over and over that he loved me and he would kiss my cheeks repeatedly and I would turn my head away, afraid that if he kissed my lips I would vomit.

One day some people from the Social Services came to see us and told my father that the state law required him to enroll me in kindergarten because I was five and too still too young for school. My father didn't like that at all, but agreed that I would start going to kindergarten and ride on the same bus that Martha and Patty rode. I was as happy as I had ever been, but I was also scared of what would be happening to me. It would be something different as I had never been anywhere without either my mother or my father. Guess you could imagine that I was a little excited.

The morning I was to start kindergarten, my father came into my room to wake me. He didn't have to call me, as I had been awake for some time, almost too excited to sleep. He helped me out of bed and began to undress me, despite me telling him that I could do it by myself. He was telling me that he wanted me to look nice for all the other people. I had taken a bath the night before so that it wouldn't take me long to get ready. I really didn't want to miss that bus. My father took me into his arms, squeezing me close to him and kissed my face, saying that he thought I would be the most beautiful girl in the class. I tried to get out of his arms so I could put my dress on, and finally he released me but then picked up my dress to put it over my head. I could feel his hands touching my body as he slid the dress down over my legs. I could hear him grunt as he released me and stood up. Then he went into the bathroom and shut the door while I finished getting dressed, put my shoes on and went into the kitchen. My bowl of oatmeal was on the table, and this morning I ate quickly so that I would be ready to go. Martha and Patty were both ready, so I guess that my father had helped them get dressed before coming into my room. He finished in the bathroom, flushing the toilet and then came out.

We heard the bus coming, so when our father opened the door, we quickly ran outside so that the bus would not leave without us. When we got in, there were about ten or twelve other kids about our ages, and that was a noisy bunch of people as everyone seemed to be talking at the same time. The driver more or less ignored the noise as she had rosebuds in her ears; I suppose she was listening to music or something. She waited until we had all sat down and put on our seatbelts before she started the bus and I was headed toward my great adventure.

Needless to say, my great adventure turned out to be my great disappointment. I'm not sure exactly what I thought it would be, but it turned out to be just a room with about twenty desks in the basement of a Baptist church. Kids sat at most of them, but there were a few empty ones. There was one adult, who turned out to be the teacher, and she told me to take one of the empty seats. The rest of the kids were about my age and I later found out that the class was for five-year-olds and there were other classes for other ages. We spent most of the days learning letters and alphabets as well as some arithmetic, most of which I already knew. I suppose the purpose of the classroom setting was to get kids accustomed to being in class and learning to follow instructions. We did get to go outside to play sometime in the middle of the morning and then we had a big surprise. Lunch. There was a eating area in the basement and the people there served us hotdogs and french-fries. That was the best lunch I had ever had. In fact it was the first hotdog and the only french-fries that I had ever eaten. My mouth wanted more, but they only served us one hotdog and a handful of french-fries. Of course, I was sad because I knew that I would not be coming back to kindergarten every day and I would not get any more of those lunches. Then, after we ate, they had us rest for a while. We had to put our heads down on our desks and pretend that we were asleep. That was okay, but I had to stand up and tell the teacher that I needed to potty. She led me down the hall to a bathroom that had four or five toilets; the biggest bathroom that I had ever seen. And there were four sinks so that four people could wash their hands at the same time. Wow.

All too soon the day came to an end and we were on the bus back home. As we went through the front door, our father picked up Patty and gave her a quick hug and a peck on the cheek. Then he put her down and picked up Martha, giving her a quick hug also and a peck on the cheek. Putting her down, he picked me up and hugged me to his chest, holding me there for what seemed to be a long time. Then he looked into my eyes and gave me a kiss. Not on the cheek, this time he gave me a rather quick peck on the lips. Then he leaned back, still holding me to his chest and looked at me for a long moment. Then, he put me back on my feet and told us that our supper would be ready in a little while. He was going to make us scrambled eggs and sausage. Then he asked us all about our day at the care center. That was the first time I believe he ever asked Martha or Patty about their class, and they just said it okay, like every other day. Then he turned to me and asked me about my day. I told him everything tht we done and about the hotdog and french-fries they had fed us.

"Did you like the hotdogs?" he asked.

"Not hotdogs, there was only one. And yes, I loved the taste and could have eaten another one if they had given it to me. But the french-fries were a little salty."

"That's the way they are supposed to be."

"Well, I think I would like them better with a little less salt."

"Well, maybe tomorrow."

"I'm going back tomorrow?"

"Yeah. Tomorrow and every day except for Saturday and Sunday."

"That's great. I'll have hotdogs every day."

My father gave me a strange look, as if he wanted a hotdog too.

"And I have some homework to do." I told him.

"What kind of homework?"

"I'm supposed to print the alphabet and numbers up to one hundred and give them to the teacher the next time that I see her."

"That's tomorrow, so you had better do you work now. If you want me to, I'll help you."

"Okay."

We moved into the kitchen so that I could use the table to write. The chairs were a little low, so when we ate, we kids had to sit on cushions to lift us up to the table. My father told me that I needed to be higher in order to write better and he sat in the chair and took me up on his lap. That raised me high enough that I could write, so I started printing my alphabets. I would do a string of the twenty-six letters and then another string of numbers from one to twenty-six. Then another string of letters and numbers twenty-seven through fifty-two, and so on until I got to one hundred numbers and twenty six letters that filled up the page. That was how my father suggested that I should do it and then he told me to repeat the whole thing again. And then again. All the time he was holding me in his lap with his hands on my legs above my knees. I thought he was just trying to keep me from falling off, as I seemed to be sitting on a lump that he had in his pocket and he would keep adjusting me from one side to another. Finally, he gave a groan sort of like a frog croaking.

"Did I hurt you?"

"No, no... you did just fine. Are you finished?"

Strange question, he saw me finish the page. "Yep."

"Then go and help your sisters."

I got off lap and headed to the bedroom where Martha and Patty had gone to play. When my father stood up, it looked like he has spilled something in his lap, his pants looked wet. Before I could ask him, he turned and went into the bathroom and closed the door. Like always, when he went to the bathroom, he locked the door. I went to my room and lay on my bed, wondering if I had done something wrong and afraid that I had. But, at the supper table, it seemed that everything was fine, my father didn't seem mad at all and joked a little with all three of us kids.

That night I woke up to a loud noise. As I lay there in my bed wondering what was going on, I could hear my mother and my father shouting at each other. Because my door was shut and their door was also shut, I couldn't hear what they were saying, but it was apparent that they were both mad and shouting. Because Martha and Patty's room was between my room and my parents, I could hear—or thought I heard my sisters crying, so I got out of bed and went into their room. Sure enough, they were awake, both in Martha's bed, hugging each other and crying. I went over to the bed to hug them both and tell them that everything was alright. Now I could hear some of that my father was shouting, "Whore! Slut! Bitch!" Then I heard a noise that sounded like somebody had slapped somebody hard, Whack! After that, there was some loud sobs and I knew it was my mother crying. I didn't know what to do, so I just stayed on the bed hugging both my sisters as the loud crying continued for a while and then everything was quiet.

"It's okay, everything will be okay. You both can go to sleep, I'll stay here with you."

It took a while but finally Patty went to sleep and Martha wasn't long behind. Although the bed was a single bed, there was space enough for three small children, so I spent the rest of the night with my sisters.

The next morning, my father woke me up by shouting, "What in the hell are you doing in this room? Why aren't you in your own bed?"

"Martha and Patty got scared last night. They heard you and Mother and the noise woke them up."

He turned away, muttering something. Then he said, "Well, get up and get ready to eat. The bus will be here soon."

His words reminded me about the wonderful lunch that I had eaten the day before, so I jumped out of bed and went to my room. I didn't even mind when my father stood in the doorway watching me as I undressed and put on new underwear. Before I could put my dress on, he came over to me, sat on the bed and pulled me between his legs. He hugged me and told me that he was sorry that he had yelled at me. Then he kissed me, just a quick peck on my lips and reached over and took my dress. He helped me put it on and again I could feel his hands rubbing on my tummy and back as he adjusted the dress so that it fit properly. Then he gave me a swat on my rear, but it wasn't too hard and didn't really hurt.

"Get in there and eat your breakfast, and help your sisters. You don't want to be late. Maybe you'll have a hotdog again today."

"I hope so. I love them."

Although Martha was only four—almost five—and Patty was three, or almost four, they both had their clothes on and were already sitting at the table eating breakfast. Guess what? Yeah, oatmeal. But our father had bought some raisins and had put some in the oatmeal. Surprisingly, that tasted pretty good, or at least it changed the taste so it wasn't so blah.

The ride on the bus and the morning in the classroom couldn't go fast enough. I was dying to get to lunch to find out if they would serve hotdogs again. I really hoped that they would, and I wasn't disappointed. In fact, the hotdog on that day tasted even better than the day before, and to tell the truth, the french-fries tasted better too. For some reason, it didn't see as if they were as salty as they had been before. I hate to admit it but I scarfed down that hotdog. I know it might have been better if I had slowly eaten the meal, but I just couldn't help myself. Actually, I was hoping that if I finished quickly, I might get a second one. But, no such luck. Still, that was a lot better than having oatmeal to eat all the time. Otherwise, it seemed that this day was the same as the day before, with the same teacher, the same rest period, the same exercise. I now know that they had worked out a routine that made the maximum use of their time with us that would keep us interested, and in hindsight appreciate the care that they took as it made it much easier for me to accept the regulations in place when I eventually entered the first grade of regular school.

Once again, our father was waiting at the front door when we kids got home. And like the day before, he gave Patty and Martha a quick hug and a peck on their cheeks, and then he picked me up. Again he held me against his chest until I could feel how warm his body was and how hard muscles were and then he kissed me on the lips again. This time, it was still a peck, but not a real quick one. Then he leaned back, still holding me with his arm under my hips and looked at me with a strange look.

"Love me?"
"Uh huh."
"Really?"
"Un huh. Yeah."

Then he gave me another kiss on my lips and put me back on my feet. "If you have any work, you had better get to doing it." He looked disappointed when I told him that they had not given us any homework.

But then he smiled and said, "You had still better practice printing your numbers and letters. You did pretty good, but I think that you can do better."

"Okay."

"Better change out of your school clothes. You will have to wear them again tomorrow."

"Okay, I'll change right now."

I didn't really notice him as he followed me to my room and stood in the doorway watching me as I changed clothes. He didn't say anything, just watched. I didn't see any reason why I should put my shoes on as I wasn't going outside, and even if I did go out, most of the time I was barefooted anyway. My mother had told me that I had to save the shoes for special occasions and I didn't need to wear them out by wearing them all the time. After changing, I went into the kitchen to practice my printing.

My father was sitting in his regular chair when I got there and he reached over and picked me up, placing me on his lap as he had the day before. He kept knees together so that I straddled his legs, one of my legs on each side. That was really more comfortable than the day before, but once again I could feel the hard ball in his pocket. It seemed to jab me whichever way I sat and I kept trying to shift around so it wouldn't hurt so much. As I printed the letters, I could hear my father breathing get a little louder, as if he was hurting. I looked back to see if he was and I saw that his eyes were closed. I didn't think he was asleep, so I just twisted back around and kept practicing. Then I heard him grunt again like had had before, and it seemed that the knob in his pocket moved away so that I didn't feel it any more.

Without saying a word, my father picked me up and set me back on my feet, stood up and walked into the bathroom, locking the door behind him. He seemed to be grumbling something, but I don't know if he was trying to talk or not. Anyway, I couldn't make out anything that he would have been saying and now that I was standing, I felt that I could go to my room and relax. I had a coloring book they had given me at the care center and wanted to try to color a picture. Although I had colored other pictures before, this was the first time that I had a full box of crayons and could pick my own colors. Most of the time I could stay inside the lines, but not always. Still, it was fun, almost like bringing the picture to life as I chose the various colors.

That night, as the night before, my mother and my father were shouting at each other and again I went into my sisters' room to be with them. This time there were more than one slap, as if someone was beating someone. Then I heard my father say, "Your face ain't been hurt, you slut, so you can keep on showing your stuff. But, bitch, you had better bring it all home to me." Then there was another slap or two, or perhaps more. And then it got quiet.

The next morning, my father was very angry at me for having spent the night in my sisters' room. "I had better not catch you in their room again," he yelled. "You stay in your own room. Those kids will be alright without you."

I started crying. That was the first time he had yelled at me. "You had better stop that crying before I give you something to cry for. You are just like your mother."

I had no idea what he meant by that, but he scared me enough that I forced myself not to cry as I turned and went into my room. This time he didn't just stand in the doorway, he came over to me and took my night gown off of me. Actually, it was just one of his tee shirts that I was using as a night gown. Then he reached over and took the edge of my panties and started pulling them down. "Lift your foot. Now the other one," he commanded as he stripped me. Then he just sat there for a while looking at me with a strange look in his eyes. Standing up, he turned toward the door and said, "Get dressed. You are late." I put my clothes on quickly because I really didn't want him to help me. For some reason, I was becoming a little scared of him although he had never done anything to me and had only yelled at me that one time.

The school—or rather the kindergarten—was becoming fun. The teacher would show us how to do different things and we began to learn words and how to add numbers. A lot of the books the teachers used had a bunch of pictures that made it easier to understand what the words we learned actually meant. Eventually we started to subtract numbers as well, but we didn't really get into much arithmetic until I entered regular school. Still, my favorite time was meal time. We didn't get hotdogs every day, but we did get them three or four times a week. Other times we would get a hamburger—they were good also, but not as good as hotdogs—or we would get a sandwich. Of all the sandwiches we got, my favorite was peanut butter and grape jelly. I bet I could have eaten ten of them, but they would only give me one. I suppose I should have been thankful, but to tell the truth, I was still hungry after eating just a sandwich and a small amount of potato chips—another new thrill for me. Like the french-fries, the potato chips were salty, but they were crunchy and I sort of liked the way they would crumble in my mouth.

That is pretty much how my early childhood days were spent. My sisters and I would go to kindergarten and then come on the bus. When we got home, our father was always at the door, picking up first Patty—I guess because she was the youngest—and then Martha, saving me for the last. When he picked up Patty or Martha, he would put his hands under their arms and lift them, give them a quick hug and a quick peck and then put them down. With me, he would put his arm under my bottom and lift me up onto his chest and then hold me there, hugging me rather tightly. Then he would kiss me on my lips only now the kisses were longer as he pressed his lips against mine for what seemed to me a long time. I really didn't mind, his lips were warm and smooth. At least I didn't mind if his breath didn't stink. Normally, it wasn't too bad at that time of the day, it only got bad later on after he had been drinking stuff from a bottle or a can.

Just as he was waiting for us every day when we got home, he and Mother seemed to argue every night and even through the double walls between our rooms I could hear him rant and rave. Most of the time I could also hear either him slap her or her as she slapped him. I didn't know which one was hitting the other, but I believed that my father was too big for my mother to hit. Anyway, I knew better than disobey him, so I remained in my room, often pulling the covers over my head and putting my head under the pillows to stifle the noises. I guess that Patty and Martha got used to the noise as I didn't hear them crying; at least, not every night.

I wasn't exactly a light sleeper, however, unusual and loud noises would wake me up. One night I woke up but didn't hear any noise. I wasn't sure what had wakened me, but it felt like someone was in the room with me. I tried to hold my breath to hear if there was anybody there; maybe a bed monster or something like that. But I didn't hear anything and didn't see anything—it was too dark and there was no nightlight. Anyway, after a while I went back to sleep and didn't wake again until my father called me to get up. When I got out of the bed, he was standing there again, as usual. He began taking my clothes off although I told him that I could do it. He ignored me, taking the tee shirt away and then my panties. As I stood there without any clothes, he put his hand on my shoulder and just let it lay there for several moments and then stood up and walked out of my room without saying a word. I finished dressing and then went out to eat breakfast. Oatmeal. Ugh. But this time it tasted pretty good. Seems like our father had gotten hold of a jar of honey and had mixed some of the honey with the oatmeal. Tasting the mixture, I decided that with this taste, I might even get to where I liked oatmeal.

Taking a break, as an adult, I can tell you frankly that if I never see oatmeal again in my lifetime, that will be too soon. You can take all of the oatmeal in the world and shove... why not send it to the starving children in South America, Africa and the Far East? Cheaper than foreign aid.

Reflecting back, it is easy to see where this was all heading, but understand that at the age of five—almost six—that I had no idea what was taking place. Of course, at that age, had I known, I'm not sure what I could have done about it. Perhaps tell someone at the kindergarten or later in school, but I don't think that anyone would have believed me. After all, what kind of a father does it take to take advantage of a five-year-old child of his own?

The daily bus rides to kindergarten, the good lunches—which I now know were free lunches donated by the church members—and the rides home almost never changed. I still ate hotdogs three or four days out of five, I still loved the taste of them and by now enjoyed the french-fries almost as much. And the hugs and kisses when I got home continued, except as time went by, the hugs got tighter and the kisses got longer. And I was still too short to reach the table without help, so I continued to sit on my father's lap and do my homework. Every time that I sat on his lap it seemed that the hard knob in his pocket would poke me in my bottom for a while as I tried to be comfortable, and then after a while, the knob would disappear. And every time that the knob disappeared, my father had to go to the bathroom. Anytime that I looked at his pants, his lap seemed to be wet. I thought maybe he was waiting too long before going to the bathroom and though about asking him if he had to go so that he wouldn't get wet, but for some reason I was afraid to talk to him about that.

Our lives never seemed to change. Mother and our father would argue and fight at night, and then it would get quiet. I learned not to try to go to sleep before their fuss took place so that I would not wake up. I guess Martha and Patty also learned. Either that or they learned to ignore it, which was more than I could do.

After the first night that I had wakened thinking that someone was in the room, I didn't have that same feeling for a while. However, after a few days—or nights—I woke up again, believing that someone was in the room with me. I had the feeling that someone—or something—had touched me, but when I woke up, I couldn't see anything in the dark and I couldn't hear anyone breathing or moving. Still, I felt certain that there was something in the room with me. I thought that perhaps it was my guardian angel sprinkling angel dust over me.

This went on night after night. After my parents finished their nightly set-to, I would go to sleep and sometime in the night, I would wake up, feeling that someone was there and that the someone had touched me. Sometimes I found that my tee shirt/night gown had ridden up, leaving my legs bare and my panties showing—that is, if anyone could see in the dark.

I can't say that it really surprised me when one night I woke up and found that my father's hand was touching my bottom, patting and caressing. "What...?"

"It's alright, honey. I had to wake you up. You were having a nightmare and yelling. I didn't want you to wake your sisters."

"Um… okay, I don't remember a nightmare."

"That's alright. Just go back to sleep. I am in the house and will protect you."

His words made me feel safe. Perhaps that had been the trouble on the other nights, a nightmare that I couldn't remember. Anyway, the feel of my father's hand, now resting on the back of my shoulders was comforting and I went back to sleep.

Over the next several nights, it seemed that my father had to wake me almost every night. I would go to sleep and then awaken to find his hand on my bottom, on my back or on my legs, stroking and patting me as if to comfort me. I didn't know what kind of nightmares I was having, but I learned that my father's caresses made me feel safer and I was glad he was there. I wasn't scared when he came into my room like I had been before.

One night I hadn't even gone to sleep when he came in and began to caress me.

"I haven't gone to sleep," I told him.

"That's okay, maybe I can help you not to have a nightmare and you can sleep better."

That made sense, so I closed my eyes and relaxed. The feel of his warm hand on my back and on my bottom felt pretty good and I knew that I was safe from harm.

After several nights like that, evidently he got tired of kneeling on the floor and began to sit on the edge of my bed. Of course, if I were asleep that would wake me up pretty quickly, but knowing it was just my father, I would go back to sleep. It wasn't long before he began to lay down beside me and then he would continue to caress me. Sometimes, he would put both arms around me and hug me close to him, breathing in my ear and sometimes just kissing the tip of my earlobe. That seemed a little too much and I tried to twist away, but he held me tight but didn't kiss me again. He did rub his hand up and down my side and across my bottom, which seemed okay.

But then as he hugged me close one night, I could feel the knob that was always in his pocket when I sat on his lap. Not knowing what it was, I asked him, "What is that hard thing?"

"It's... er... it's my hotdog."

"You have a hotdog?"

"Yes, honey. I have a hotdog. All men have hotdogs."

"I don't have a hotdog."

"No, sweetie, only boys and men have hotdogs."

"That's not fair. Girls should have hotdogs as well."

"Well, it may not be fair, but that's the way it is."

"Why?"

"There are reasons, but we're not going to get into them tonight. You just lay here and go to sleep."

"Can I see your hotdog."

"Not tonight. Maybe some other time."

"Why?"

"It's not right."

"Why?" I heard him grunt.

"It just isn't."

"Can I touch it?"

"NO!. Just lie there and be quiet."

"Why can't I see it or touch it?"

"Because it's not right, it's just not right. Now you just lie there and shut up and go to sleep."

"But..."

"Be quiet. You go to sleep and I'll go back to my bed."

"Well, okay. But you promised some day."

He groaned again, as if something was hurting him. I started to ask him what was hurting, but he told me, "Just go to sleep."

That pretty much ended the conversation. I don't remember him getting up out of my bed, but when I woke up, I was alone and he was in the kitchen, making a lot of noise and getting breakfast ready. You've guessed it; oatmeal, but oatmeal with honey and raisins both. Yummy.

For several nights after that, my father did not come into my room, at least I don't think that he did. I would lie awake, waiting for him to come, but he didn't show up. During the day when I would try to ask him about hotdogs, he just told me to keep quiet, it wasn't something that I needed to know, that he would explain everything later. But I kept pestering him, wanting to know if only boys had hotdogs, where did the ones come from that the church school served. Did they cut them off of boys, and if they did, did the boys grow a new one? There were a lot of questions that I wanted to asked, but the look on my father's face when I started to ask one of the questions scared me so much that I didn't ask. And of course, my mother was either at work or in the bed asleep. I only saw her a little in the evening when she would get up, eat whatever my father had cooked, and then leave. I did notice that her clothes seemed to be newer and lot of colors and they fit her tighter than my clothes fit me.

Almost every day just as she was leaving my father would tell her, "You better bring some home tonight if if you know what is good for you."

She would look at him as if she was afraid of him and just nod her head as she walked out the door. "Slutty bitch whore." I heard my father mutter as she closed the door behind her.

Things seemed to get better around the house. There was more to eat and sometimes we had snacks of potato chips and popcorn as well as a candy bar from time to time. I guess at the time I believed that it was because of the money that my father was receiving from the Veterans Administration, but now I realize why my mother wore the kind of clothes she wore and where she got the money to buy them. And of course my father knew and he was making sure that she brought the money home to him. And if there wasn't enough, then he would beat her. Nonetheless, at the age of five—almost six—a child knows that something is going on, but is too naïve to understand.

My father became more and more grouchy, shouting at us kids as well as our mother. He seemed to always be angry except for the times he would help me with my homework. He would still pick me up and put me on his lap so that I could work on the table. And sure enough, that knot would always be there. I couldn't understand why the hotdogs we got in school were soft and his was always hard. I suppose at the time I thought it might be just because his was older.

One night about a month before my sixth birthday, I woke to find my father had returned to my bedroom and was running his hand up and down my legs. I didn't say anything. In fact, I was pretty glad because I thought that I might be reason that he was always angry, but now it seemed that he was okay, humming quietly as he patted my rear and then my legs again.

After a few nights, he began laying on my bed while he petted me. I didn't mind because he didn't say anything, just stroked me. Some of the nights I could feel his hard hotdog pushing against my thigh, but I didn't want to mention it because he might get mad again. There were times when he would put hand under my tee shirt nightgown and stroke my back or my shoulders or my belly. He never pinched or hit, it was just like he was petting a dog or something. I didn't mind because, after several minutes, I would go to sleep while his had hand was still on me.

One morning I woke up to find my panties down around my knees. I didn't know how they got there, but they were a little large for me and probably scooted down as I turned in the bed. The next night the same thing happened and it became a regular occurrence so I didn't think much about it. Then one morning I woke up to find that my panties were all the way off and were there in the bed at my feet. That seemed strange, they weren't that loose and anyway there was a big safety pin holding them. Still, I didn't think too much about it, believing that I may have pushed them off with my feet.

My father continued to come into my bedroom, lie on my bed and caress me. One night, when he was rubbing his hand on my rear end, he slid his hand inside my panties and I could feel his hand on my bare skin. I didn't much like that and started to twist away, but he pushed me down on the bed and told me just to be still, that everything was alright. I still was afraid to make him mad, so I did as he said.

Now it seemed that his knob, or his hotdog, pushed against me every night. I still didn't move away, and although I was curious, I didn't dare touch it or say anything to him. I would just lay there and keep quiet. Most of the time I would go to sleep while his hand was still on my rear, but sometimes I would hear him get out of my bed and go into the bathroom. I don't know if he ever came back into my room after that because I was always asleep by then.

One night, I could feel something wet touching my leg. The wet spot was just where his hotdog was, only now the hotdog wasn't hard and I couldn't feel it poking me, just a wet spot. I started to put my hand down there to find out why it was wet, but when my hand touched his pajama pants he grabbed my wrist. "I told you never to touch me." He was mad.

"Okay. I'm sorry."

He didn't say anything else, just got out of my bed and left the room. I could still feel a little dampness on my leg where something had touched it. I was certain that my father had peed in his pants and that was what got my leg wet. He should have gone to the bathroom earlier.

The next night my father didn't come into my room while I was awake, but the night after he did. The same thing happened on several different nights where my leg would get wet and then my father would get up and go into the bathroom. Even at night he would lock the door behind him. I didn't understand that because our mother was at work, my sisters were asleep and I wasn't going to go into the bathroom while he was there. I knew that would really make him mad.

On my sixth birthday we had a small cake with six candles. I blew them all out with one breath, so I knew that I would get my wish. But I didn't know anything to wish for, so all I got was a hug from my two sisters and a hug and a long kiss from my father. My mother couldn't bother to get out of bed, so she slept through my birthday party.

"Don't worry about it, Jeannie"—that's what my father called me when he was in a good mood—"I'll have a surprise for you later."

"What is it?"

"It's a surprise, you will find out later tonight."

Of course, I was impatient, but happy and gave him a hug. He hugged me back and kissed me hard on my lips. I didn't really like that because his breath smelled bad and his lips tasted sour.

Despite his promise and my anxiety, I didn't get a surprise before it was time for bed. I thought maybe he had forgotten and I was afraid to remind him. I didn't want him yelling at me and I was afraid that if he were mad that he might spank me. Although he had never spanked me, I had heard from other kids in my class that if they misbehaved they would get a spanking either with a hand, a paddle or a belt. So, I tried to be careful and not get in trouble with him. Finally, giving up, I took my bath and put on my tee shirt and went to bed.

Not long afterwards, while I was still lying there awake wondering why he had forgotten my present, he came in to my bedroom. I could hear him breathing as he got close to my bed and then lay down beside me. Reaching over, he pulled me over and cuddled me close. "I bet you think I forgot your surprise." His breath still smelled sour. "I didn't."

"But where is it?"

"Give me your hand." He took hold of my wrist and moved my hand down to the top of his pajamas. Then he pushed my hand into his pajamas and said, "Reach down a little further."

I did as he said and then I felt something different. It was long and round and hot. "That's my hotdog. You said that you wanted to touch it, so go ahead. You are getting old enough to learn some stuff."

My fingers touched his hotdog. "Wrap your fingers around it and feel how soft and warm it is."

It really wasn't soft, although not as hard as I had thought. And it was warm. There were hairs around one end and when I wrapped my fingers around it, he gave a lurch and then I felt my hand get all wet. He groaned loudly so I jerked my hand away. "No, that's alright, you can touch it."

"But it's wet. And it's sticky, too."

"It'll wash off, so just go into the bathroom."

While I was washing my hand, he stood in the doorway watching me. After I finished, he went into the bathroom and locked the door. I went to bed and went to sleep, wondering why my hand had gotten wet and why it had been so sticky. Pee pee didn't get sticky like that.

During the summer my father took me to the South Charlotte Elementary School to enroll me in the first grade. Although the school was a lot larger than the one at the church, I saw a few of my classmates and didn't feel scared. In fact, I was really excited because after kindergarten ended, so did my lunch of hotdogs and french-fries. We never had them at home.

That night my father came into my room just after I went to bed. He came over and told me that he was going to teach me something new. The next thing I knew he was holding my head and I could feel something at my lips.

"Open up. And don't bite it or I'll beat you."

Without becoming obscene, it's difficult to explain what happened next. As you can surmise, that was my introduction to oral sex. I didn't like it at all, it tasted bad and when his semen erupted, I just couldn't help it. I vomited. Most of it went on my bed but some splashed on him and he slapped my face really hard. I started crying, that had hurt a lot.

"Shut up that crying. If you wake your sisters, I'll beat you. Anyway, you aren't hurt. You only did what women are supposed to do for men."

I was able to stop crying, but couldn't stop sobbing. My cheek really burned and my mouth tasted awful.

"Just lay there and go to sleep." He went into the bathroom and locked the door. I was going to wait until he finished and then go in and wash my face and my mouth and get rid of that terrible taste, but he was in there so long that I went to sleep. The next morning when I went into the bathroom to wash, there was something like dried paste on my nose, my cheeks and my chin. It had also dropped down onto my throat, so I just took a full bath.

When I went into the kitchen to eat breakfast, my father looked at me and grinned. "How did you like your taste of my hotdog?"

"It tasted awful."

"You'll get used to it. You will like it. All women do."

He was wrong, I never got used to it and I never did like it. In fact, I thought it was nasty and to force a child to do that should result in the death penalty... or at least castration. That was something I thought a lot about. What if someone cut it off, would they make a meal out of it. And I believe that my father lied to me. It didn't taste anything like the hotdogs that the church school had fed us.

Anyway, the molestation continued, night after night. I thought it would never end. And if I had known how it would end, I would have preferred to continue. But I didn't know, but was soon to find out.

My first day of school was neat. I enjoyed seeing three kids from the church school who were in my first grade class, so I didn't feel like they were all strangers. I don't know how many kids were in the class, somewhere around twenty to thirty, but the day went by so fast, it didn't seem to take long at all. The bus we rode on was a large yellow bus, much bigger than the one that took us to kindergarten. Now, however, I was riding the bus alone, as Martha and Patty were still too young to go to regular school. I had homework to do, but my father had begun to have me sit on a pillow to be able to work in the table. I was glad of that because I was beginning to hate his hotdog.

He told me that he would have another surprise for me later that night. I was a little afraid, after all, his prior surprise wasn't a good one and I feared that this one wouldn't be any better. My worst fears were realized, it definitely was not better.

When I went to bed, I only put on my tee shirt nightgown as my father had forbidden me to wear panties in bed. I didn't know why, but I did know that he liked to pet my bare rear and the panties just got in his way. At any rate, he ordered and I had to obey. After a long while, I sensed that he was in my bedroom again, and sure enough, he lay down beside me. As he rolled me over on my side to cuddle me, I could feel his bare skin; he was naked.

Then he took the hem of the tee shirt and lifted it over my head and took it off. I heard it hit the floor and was too scared to move. Now I was completely naked and so was he. He began to kiss my face and my neck. Then he put his lips on mine and forced my mouth open. I felt him stick his tongue in my mouth and it tasted worse than the oatmeal, almost as bad as his semen. Then he rolled me over onto my back and then got between my legs, forcing them wide apart. He said, "Now you are going to learn what a woman is good for."

I felt him probing my private parts and wanted to tell him to stop, but his mouth was smothering mine so I couldn't make any noise. Then I felt him put something in my private parts and then he pushed hard and really hurt me. I had never felt such pain and have not felt any thing that hurt as much in my entire life. It was like he had stuck me with a knife and it was tearing me apart. I tried and tried to escape, to twist my body away from him, but he was too heavy and too strong for me. Then everything got black and I guess that I fainted. I don't know what happened after that. The next morning when I woke up, I hurt so bad in my privates that I couldn't move. I felt something on my stomach and my legs that had dried and when I could finally move the bedcovers and sit up, I could see that it looked like catsup or tomato paste, but dark red and dried hard. I knew I would have to get up and wash it off, but somehow I just couldn't move, it hurt too much. When I tried to move my legs to the side of the bed, the pain caused me to faint again.

I heard my father come to the door of my bedroom, but I kept my eyes closed, hoping that he would just leave me alone. He must have known I was awake because he told me to get up and wash, that it would make me feel better. Knowing that I didn't dare disobey, I finally was able to get to my feet, but the pain was so much that I could barely walk. I took tiny baby steps toward the bathroom because it hurt too much to try to take a step.

My father watched as I inched my way to the bathroom and told me that the hurt would go away. He also said that I would soon get to where I liked it as much as my mother. Realizing that he meant to do it again, I was so scared that I began to vomit and couldn't help myself. It hurt so much I couldn't run to the bathroom and I vomited on the floor. He just laughed and told me to clean it up after I took my bath.

When I got in the bathtub, the warm water felt pretty good, but I noticed that I was bleeding a little from my private parts. What had happened is that he had torn me I a couple of places and blood was seeping out of me into the water. After I soaked for a while, I could move a little easier, but I had to crawl out of the bathtub. It still hurt too much to stand up straight. Nevertheless, my father insisted that I clean up the floor and the bathroom. He told me that I was finally a woman and that I would be able to please a man, since that was what women were created to do. "Otherwise," he said, "women are not good for anything."

For the next couple of nights he left me alone, for which I was very glad. If he had tried to do it again, I really believe that it would have killed me. Even so, the reprieve didn't last very long, because a few nights later, he was back in my room. Although he promised that it wouldn't, it hurt just as much as it did the first time, or maybe even worse. But with his mouth smothering mine, I couldn't scream or anything. He told me that if I made a lot of noise and woke my sisters that he would beat me and them as well. I still would have screamed if I had been able, I don't think I could have held it back. I bled again, but it didn't seem to be as much blood this time as the first.

Soon it became an every night thing. I would go to bed and as soon as Martha and

Patty were asleep, he would come in and put his thing in me. He kept telling me that this was the only reason God had made women, and that otherwise, we were just no damn good at all. He told me that my mother was spreading it all over town so he was going to keep me for his own, that I would take her place. After he would leave me, I would cry for a while, get up and wash myself, then cry myself to sleep.

Although I was now tall enough to sit on a chair—with a small cushion—and work on the tabletop, there were many occasions that my father would make me sit on his lap and do my work. He would put his hand on my private parts, move my panties aside, and stick his finger in me. He would move it around in me and tell me how much I was going to learn to enjoy that. Truth is, it hurt almost as much as thing did and I never learned to enjoy it.

I suppose you are wondering why I didn't tell anyone at school what was happening. That was because my father sat me down one day and talked to me. He told me that he wasn't supposed to be doing what h e was doing and that if I told anybody, he might have to leave and take his money with him. In that case, we would lose the house and it was likely that Martha and Patty would be put in foster homes and I would never see them again. He also said that if I refused to do it with him, he would have to go on to Martha or Patty or both. I knew how much it hurt me and was afraid that it would kill my sisters, so I just kept my mouth shut and didn't tell anyone for a while. There was one day that I was at the table when my mother came into the kitchen, sat down with a cup of coffee and asked me how everything was going. Having just been hurt again by my father the night before, I told her that my father was doing things to me. She sat her coffee cup on the table, reached over and slapped me hard enough to make the tears flow. She told me that she didn't believe me, that my father was not that kind of man, and that I should not tell lies like that. She told me that if I told anybody else something like that, she would see that I was placed in an orphanage and that my sisters would be taken away. I kept crying but she didn't care. She sat there, drank the rest of her coffee, then got up and went into her room, got dressed and left.

Of course, with all the threats and the idea of my sisters being taken away from me, I kept quiet and never let anybody know what was going on. In fact, I didn't let Martha or Patty know what was going on either, as I didn't want them to get into trouble or have our father do to them what he was doing to me. This situation remained the same until I was in the eighth grade, and was almost fourteen. The one thing that changed was that when I was ten he had taken me to the doctor and asked the doctor to put me on the pill as he was afraid that I might be a little promiscuous. The doctor never asked me a question, just gave my father the prescription and said that I needed to be seen once a year. And that was it. Ten years old and on the pill. Isn't that a blast?

Just before I graduated the eighth grade, my father told me that he had another surprise for me. Knowing him, I was sure it would be a stinker, but what was I to do? Not only did he control me, but he had the threat of causing damage to my younger sisters and he knew how much I loved them. The fact that I had taken care of them when he was still in the Army almost made them the same as my own children and there wasn't and still isn't anything that I wouldn't do for them.

After we went through the graduation ceremony, my father drove that old car back to our house and told Martha to take Patty and go in the house and that he and I would be back later. Martha was almost thirteen and our father felt that she was old enough to take care of Patty for a while.

What I didn't know was what lay ahead, and if I had known, I believe that I would have run in the house and locked the door so he couldn't get in. He must have felt that I would bolt, because he took a tight grip on my arm and held me in the care until my sisters had gotten out and closed the door. Then he drove away and we went to a building somewhere down the road quite a ways. When we got to the building, he got out and told me to get out. I knew that I had to obey, but thought that although I might be in trouble, there wasn't much he could do out in public. Someone might see.

Taking me by the arm, he took me to a door, opened the door and led me inside. It seemed that this was a clubhouse, with ping-pong tables, a pool table, a bunch of chairs and sofas. There wasn't anybody there except for us at first and then a door opened and two men came through. I didn't know them but they evidently knew my father, shouting hello and hey.

My father said to them that he had promised them something worth the money and here it was. That scared me and I whirled around to run, but it was too late. My father grabbed me, and although I was a good bit larger, I wasn't large enough to get away. The other men also came over and one of them took one of my arms while the second man took the other. They dragged me over to one of the sofas, my father helping, and then stretched me out on the sofa. One of the men unbuttoned my dress while the other man took off my shoes and socks, and then reached up and grabbed my panties. Rather than taking them off, he just ripped them away. I don't think I have to tell you what happened next, but the three of them just kept doing it over and over and over. I lost track of how many or who was doing it when because I kept blacking out and coming to and then blacking out again. After what seemed like hours, they either got too tired or to spent to do anything further so they let me loose.

My father told me to put my clothes back on and that he would take me home. It was all that I could do to get back to the car and when we got home, I just fell on my bed although it was not yet night. Now I realize that at the time it seemed odd. I thought the rape had taken much longer, but it was still light when my father took me home. I didn't get out of bed until after noon the next day.

That event did change things for me. I decided that if my father could let someone do that to me, I could let anybody I chose to do the same. I wasn't getting any pleasure, only pain, but had heard that it would feel good if you did it with someone you liked. In truth, there weren't that many guys that I liked but there were a couple of cute boys in my class. But I wasn't just going to hand out for nothing. There is a say ing, WIIIFM—what is in it for me. If they were going to get into my pants, there had to be something in it for me. And there was. Have you ever tried Mary Jane? Oh, you know, marijuana? Pot? Let me tell you that it makes things better. That was my price. One joint of pot for one turn. Pay up in advance, no credit.

It didn't take long for word to get around. I'm not sure that I took on everybody in the entire high school system, but if they had a joint, then they had a chance. But, nothing free. In the southern part of Charlotte at the time, there was still sufficient open space and wooded land that you could find a space where no one would see you. And anyway, it didn't take those young boys that long to get off. Wham, Bam, Thank You Man.

As my skills grew, so did my ability to hide my operations from my father and from my sisters. I didn't think that anyone knew anything about what I was doing, but I reckoned without my sisters, who were learning things in school that I would rather have not had them know. Still...

My tastes were also changing. Pot was okay, but most of it had been cut so much that you could only get a slight lift, not the high that I was looking for. Checking around, I found other options and as I did so, the price for 'my favors' also changed. Instead of a joint of marijuana, I began getting stronger stuff—they called it 'shit'—and I was able to continue to get high enough that I didn't care what the boys did to me. I didn't enjoy it, but they did. I did, however, enjoy their little 'gifts' to me, often dozing off even as they were doing their thing. Oxycotton and other narcotics were able to lull me while the guys had their fun. While it didn't take them too long, the buzz often lasted all afternoon, or at least for a couple of hours.

Unfortunately, the use of narcotics led me to become a little careless. One of the guys or my father or one of his friends—there had been a goodly number after the first two—was evidently more viral than he thought or it could be that I just forgot the pills intentionally, but I became pregnant before I was sixteen years old. That really set my father off, although if I had known how upset he would be, I might have gotten pregnant earlier. Still, I didn't want to make him so angry that he would turn to my sisters. At the time I was completely unaware that he had already got to Martha and was getting ready for Patty. I had read enough books to know that it was relatively simple to cause a miscarriage, and had even read on YouTube about some girl doing it herself with just a coat hanger. Well, I had a coat hanger, and if she could... That didn't turn out too well. The coat hanger did its job, alright, and in fact did it all too well. There was a lot of blood, and I was afraid that I would be dying. Although I tried to stop the bleeding with a towel, the blood soaked through and when my father saw how much I was bleeding, he told me to get in the car. I did so and he drove me to the hospital. There he told me to get out and go in and see the doctor. As I went through the doors to the emergency room, I heard him drive away. I started to cry because he didn't care enough to get out and stay with me. Now I was alone and didn't know what to do. However, the people on duty at the emergency room certainly knew; they had me on a bed and in a room in a matter of minutes. Then someone came in and gave me a shot in the arm and I don't remember anything else until I woke up the next day.

The people at the hospital kept asking me what my name was and I finally told them that I was Evelyn Meadows. When they asked my address, I gave them the address of the kindergarten and when they asked me how old I was, I told them that I was twenty-two. I don't know if they believed me or not, as they looked a little skeptical, but I kept up the falsehood until the doctor told me that I was ready to be released. After the nurse brought my clothes, I dressed while she went for a wheelchair. I didn't wait, but sneaked out and left the hospital without signing out. I did take the prescription that the doctor had given me. It was for Valium and would come in handy as the pain would come and go. There was no one home when I got there, so I just crawled through the window to my bedroom, which I left open to get fresh air. I curled up on the bed and the next thing I knew was Martha waking me up to find out what had happened. Of course, I didn't tell her the truth, in fact, by this time I was becoming quite an accomplished liar. I'll tell you one thing; I never again forgot to take the birth control pill, although as I was to find out several years later the aborted abortion had negated the possibility of my ever getting pregnant again. Even if I had known that, I would still have taken the pill because it just hurt too damn bad to go through all that again.

At the age of sixteen, I quit school and ran away to move in with a boy that I found pretty cute. He had a part time job and was making pretty good money as a mechanic in a garage on Arrowhead Boulevard. I was certain that I was in love and would live with him forever. Then, all of a sudden, the police found me. They arrested me and took me to the precinct and notified my father that I was in custody. My father came to get me and told me that if I ran away again, he would keep Martha and Patty and make them sex toys for him and his friends. That got my attention, so I promised not to run away again. He would continue to use me for the next two years, until I was eighteen and found a boy who wanted to marry me.

I decided to tell my sisters what had been happening to me, and was completely shocked to know that my father had also raped both my sisters on repeated occasions. He had even taken both of them to the clubhouse where his friends had raped me. There he had given them alcohol and drugs and his friends had had a party on more than one occasion.

My father doesn't know how lucky he was. If he had been home at that time, I would have taken a butcher knife and killed him and cut his 'hotdog' off at the roots. In fact, even today, if I had the chance, I would cut it off and feed it to him while he was still alive. And I bet Martha and Patty might just help.

Okay, I'm about finished with my part of the story. The boy that I did finally marry must have felt that the grass is greener on the other side of the fence. After we had been married for about four years, he began seeing a girl more than six year younger than he was, still in her teens. Guess he thought she was more pure than I. I would like to say it hurt a lot, but in truth that would be a lie. I did like Jerry, but was only fond of him. I really wasn't in love with him at all; it was just that he was always nice to me. Anyway, I hope him the best now that he is on his third wife. The teenager only lasted a little more than two years. I lasted longer... is that snide?

Well, maybe someday Mr. Right will come along. I wouldn't bet on it, but until he does, I'm keeping my legs crossed. Since I never had any pleasure in doing it, I don't see any reason for keep on doing it unless you find the right one. So far, I haven't. But I am still looking.

Ciao.

Martha Sue

As I sit here listening for the second time in my life to Shirley Jean tell you all about her childhood, my mind can't help but flash back to the events of my own childhood that I can remember. I was a little younger than she and Shirley Jean did a good job of hiding her ordeal from me so I really wasn't aware of what was happening to her; I only knew about the things that happened to me. Even more regretful, I didn't know what my younger sister Patty was to experience. I'm not sure what I could have done about it, but I would like to think that there may have been something that would have stopped the monster that we knew as our father. And that is exactly what he was, a monster that preyed on young children. I can only hope and pray that he limited his depraved activities to the three of us and that the other young, innocent children out there were not harmed by his evil attention.

I am now aware that he had been injured during the war and that the injury to his head may have changed his personality. And now they tell us a lot about Post-traumatic Stress Disorder, which is a devilish mental problem that many veterans suffer. I don't believe that even our mother would have married a man like that.

I'm not really sure exactly when it began, but by the time that I was eight, I noticed that my father's hugs were getting tighter and longer. Even more, he would hug me when no one else was around, and then he would kiss me on the top of my head and my forehead. I thought that was nice, it was good to have a parent that loved me because my mother was never around. It was almost like she was ashamed of having children, so she more or less ignored us. That was okay because Shirley Jean would take care of us and make sure that we were clean and that we ate. Of course, like she said, the only thing she had to feed us was oatmeal, but that was okay because I really loved the taste of oatmeal. Even when there was no milk and Shirley Jean had to make the oatmeal with water, it still tasted pretty darn good to me. I always cleaned my plate and if Shirley Jean or Patty left any on their plate, I would finish that as well.

Today is only the second time that I have heard my sister Shirley Jean's story. It will be the first time I have ever heard Patty speak about our childhood. And it will be the first time that they have heard my story as well. It seems that as kids, we were careful to keep certain things private when in fact we should have been telling each other and the world at large what was going on behind closed doors. As I listened to Shirley Jean tell how our father raped her for the first time, it actually brings the pain that I suffered, a pain almost too much for a child to suffer. If a man had to go through the same ordeal, he would probably cut his organ off before he would suffer like that.

My father didn't actually attack me in my bed. I was sharing the room with Patty and I guess that he just didn't want to make any noise and wake her up. Like he did with Shirley Jean, he would sneak into our bedroom, which was black as ink, and run his hands up and down my body. Unlike my two sisters, I always slept nude as I didn't like to feel anything tight on me when I was trying to sleep.

At first, I felt that it was my imagination that someone was touching me, but over a period of time, I was able to wake up and catch the hand that was touching me. Although it was really, really dark, I knew that the hand was that of my father. It was too big for my sisters or my mother. Just why he was touching me wasn't clear, but it didn't seem to be hurting or anything, so I would just lay there until I would go back to sleep.

I can't tell you how long this continued, but it seems like it took place every night. Eventually I became used to the feel and some nights I didn't even wake up, so I don't know if he was there on those nights or not. I am a pretty good sleeper and don't normally wake up unless the noise is so loud that it scares me or unless someone shakes me.

The hand that would rub over me touched my chest, my hair, my face, my shoulders and my legs. The hand would also touch my rear if I were on my stomach or would touch my privates if I were on my back. Sometimes, if I were on my side, the hand would cause me to roll over one way or the other and then touch me. One night I woke up to find that I was on my back and the hand was on my privates and something was sticking into my private parts. It wasn't big and didn't go in too far, so there was no pain. There was a little discomfort, but I didn't think it was worth moving, as the hand would just move me back, so I lay there and soon was asleep again.

Over a period of time—I can't tell you how long, but it seemed a long while—the hand continued playing with my private parts, sometimes sticking something in me and sometimes just petting me there. And at times, I would hear my father make a noise, sort of a grunt or something. It was never loud and didn't seem to be painful, so I guess it was alright.

One night as I lay there drowsily, I felt the hand touch my private parts. After a minute or so, I could tell that my father was standing over my bed. He reached down, removed the covers and picked me up. I could feel his skin against mine, not realizing that he had taken his clothes off. I didn't know what he was going to do, but he began to give my face soft kisses and he began to walk. He carried me into his bedroom. This was a place where we kids had been forbidden to enter, but since he carried me in, I guess it was alright. There was a small light on a table by the bed, just enough light to see a little. Mostly, I could just see shadows. When I looked at my father, he began to kiss my lips. His lips were mashed against mine and he laid me down on the bed, and then got in beside me. He kept kissing me and kissing me and then he got to his knees and moved between my legs.

All I can tell you is that Shirley Jean didn't do half a job in describing the pain that followed. It was so sharp and so severe that I couldn't breathe; I couldn't yell, I couldn't scream. Even if I could have gotten my breath, his mouth mashed my lips flat and his tongue was in my mouth and about half way down my throat. If I had had time,

I would have gagged, but I suppose there is some safety mechanism in us that causes us to black out or faint if the pain is too severe. And you better believe that I did black out or faint or fell unconscious, say it as you will.

Talk about hell. That doesn't even begin to describe the pain. I think that it must have been equal to what Christ felt when they nailed him to the cross. Certainly, it was no less intolerable. Somehow, words just do not describe the pain and there is no way to make anyone who has never experienced it understand the sheer agony that the body feels as it is torn apart. And that is exactly what takes place and what took place, my body was torn apart.

Sore, god, I was sore as could be the next day. My father had carried me back to my bed after he had finished using me and I just lay there. I couldn't get up to go to school and that was the first day I had ever missed in preschool, kindergarten or school.

I was proud of my perfect attendance and gotten gold stars from all my teachers for always being there. Now that record was broken, and to tell the truth, I didn't care. I just hurt too much.

In the romance magazines and love story books, the sexual act is displayed as being a sweet, tender moment when love overcomes all and passion wipes away the pain. That isn't how it works when you have been raped. There is no pleasure, no love, no tenderness, no passion. There is only pain and more pain, and even more pain. It grows and grows and doesn't stop, only fading away a little at a time over a period of time. For me it took almost a week before I could walk normally without feeling like someone had put a knife into my lower belly. Now that I have learned that Shirley Jean and Patty both went through the same thing, I wonder how they stood it. I hurt so bad I wished that I would die so it would quit hurting. I can now understand why someone would commit suicide rather than facing a life of pain. I know that I would do the same.

I didn't really feel any stigma about what had happened. There was no one to tell me that it was right or wrong, I only knew that it hurt so bad that it couldn't be the right thing to do. Nothing that hurts so badly can be right.

I was surprised to hear that our father took Shirley Jean down to his clubhouse. I thought that I was the only one that he did that to, and I hate him even more now that I know just how evil he was. And he is even worse than you think as he gave all of his daughters to his 'friends' and companions to use as sex objects. I suspect that he received favors in return and probably even money, as all of a sudden he seemed to have all of the money that he needed. In fact, he had so much that he was able to trade the old Cadillac in on a newer car, a white Ford sedan. Sometimes on the way to his clubhouse he would pull off to the side of the road, make me take off my panties and have intercourse with me before continuing on to the clubhouse. It seemed to make him happy but really didn't mean a lot to me.

Like my older sister, my father took me to the doctor when I was ten and got me a prescription for birth control pills. I hadn't yet started menstruating, and couldn't get pregnant, but he didn't want to take a chance. He was very careful with me at the doctor's office, taking the position of a caring, loving father, but watching to make sure that I didn't tell anyone what he was doing to us. He didn't have to worry. I was too frightened of him to say anything to anyone and I was also afraid that if I told him to stop or if I told on him, that he would just attack Patty. I didn't know that he already had plans for her and was working on that.

At school, I learned about the reputation that Shirley Jean had gained, but I had absolutely no interest in sharing what

I had with any of the boys in my class, nor in any of the guys in the school. They all seemed to stutter and turn red when they tried to talk to me and I didn't want some stupid boy hanging around me. I knew that they would all like me to do the same thing that Shirley Jean liked to do, but I had decided that I wouldn't do so. I had read enough books to understand that there can and should be some emotion between a man and a woman, and that the emotion can be a good thing, if it is shared. I had also read enough to know that what my father was doing to his daughters was rape, illegal and immoral. Still, I didn't have the strength to tell him no, and was grateful that he seemed to want to do it less and less as time goes by. According to the books I read, the sex drive in men decreases as they grow older and I was hoping that was what was happening to my father. In fact, I wanted him to grow very old very quickly, even to die. What I didn't learn from those books was that when a man gets tired of one woman, he is apt to turn to another, fresher woman or girl, and my father was turning away from me to Patty, a year younger and a year fresher.

In my junior year of high school, I met Steve. Steve was my idea of what a man should be like. He stood about six feet tall, was lean but not skinny, was cute, but not *cute.* He was very polite with me, a little shy and quiet. He didn't seem to grab or to paw, but was quietly reserved. Still, I could tell from his eyes that he was interested, but it didn't seem that he was just interested in getting into my pants. When he asked me to go out to a movie, I agreed. Steve was seventeen, had his driver's license and could borrow his parents' car. On the way to the movie house, he kept his hands on the steering wheel and his eyes—most of the time—on the road. During the movie, he did put his arm around my shoulder, but didn't squeeze nor try hug me or kiss me. I thought that was nice and it gave me a warm and fuzzy feeling.

That feeling didn't last too long. When Steve walked me up to my front door, before he could say anything or try to kiss me, the door was jerked open and my father was standing there, looking dirty, rough and unshaven. He told me to get into the house right now and told Steve that I was too young to go out with him alone, that he should wait until I was eighteen. Steve left without arguing and I went into the house.

No sooner was I inside than my father took me by the arm and literally dragged me into his bedroom, throwing me on his bed. He lifted my skirt and ripped off my panties, a new pair that I had worn that night just in case. Without a word and without taking off his pants he threw himself on me and rammed his thing into me. He kept going on and on and on and I thought it would never end. But finally he gave out and fell over to one side. I was able to get out from under him and went into my room, leaving him lying there all tired out. When I got into my room I noticed there was no sperm or anything, evidently my father was to drunk or too tired to ejaculate, but I still went into the bathroom and washed myself, scrubbing hard trying to wash his stink off of me.

I didn't give up seeing Steve, but I did make arrangements to meet him away from my house. We would go to a movie, or maybe have a 'shake and fries, or sometimes just walk around. Other times we would go to the mall, sit on one of the benches, and talk until the mall closed. Don't ask me what we talked about, I really can't remember. It wasn't much of substance, just what we would like to do in the future, what we wanted to study, what kind of work we wanted to do, where it would be nice to live, what kind of family would be nice to have. We found that we both loved the mountains, but we also found that we both loved the seashore or the lakeside, such as the one between Charlotte and South Carolina. That was an area where my father would take us to play when we were younger and when he was in a good mood. That is, if he had enough money to buy gas for that old Cadillac that he had. We kids loved to play in the warm sand and then wash our bare feet in the cool water.

Over a period of time, Steve and I came to understand each other better. He didn't have any idea of what was happening in my home, but he knew there was some anger between my father and me. He just didn't know just how deep that anger ran and that it was me that was angry with my father. Steve could feel some of the heat in the rare instances that I talked about my father, because I tried my best not to talk about him at all and would only answer Steve's questions about him in as few words as possible.

I guess I am quite a lot like Shirley Jean and Patricia Ann. Somehow it was never Mom or Mommy or Momma and it was never Dad or Daddy or Poppa. Pet names like those are reserved for the ones you love and the ones that you respect and not for the ones that you hate and that you detest. It just doesn't seem fitting.

The more I saw of Steve, the more I grew to like him. It wasn't anything hot and romantic, like you read about in some of the novels that are popular. It was more of getting accustomed to each other, learning what the other is thinking about, judging each other's temperature and keeping everything cool. We would go on dates to movies and the like, we would often hod hands, and we would sometimes kiss. No, not the heavy-breathing french-kissing, but pleasant, nice, feel-good kissing and companionship that seemed to make my home life even more unendurable. It also made life with Steve look even better. As you might expect, he did eventually propose to me and asked me if I would marry him.

What could I do? Of course, I said yes. Steve was a nice guy and I was certain that I could enjoy a long life with him. He was the first person to treat me as a human being, other than my two sisters, and he had earned my respect and admiration. I sincerely believed that would be more important than any hot passion such as may be found in the novellas.

Needless to say, the day that I was eighteen, Steve and I were standing in front of a justice of peace and two witnesses. The witnesses had been provided by the justice of peace and were two members of his family. Neither Steve nor I had even thought about witnesses. I guess that we presumed that a marriage license was all that we needed, and we had obtained that. Within a few moments and with a few words, Steve and I were "man and wife."

Taking Steve's father's truck, we drove to my house to get my clothes. I was shocked when we drove up to find most of my belongings piled up on the front porch and a note that read, "Get out and stay out, you slut."

Although I tried to keep my head up as Steve and I loaded my stuff into the truck and drove toward Steve's house, I finally broke down several miles from my house and began to wail and cry. I was hysterical and couldn't stop although Steve was holding me tightly in his arms and caressing my head. I just cried and cried and cried. I know that I slobbered all over him and his clothes and I must have made him as wet as a rain shower. Finally, the crying fit ended with a bunch of hiccups and sobs.

Finally, I was able to look Steve in the face and I knew that I must have looked a mess. There was a bit of shock in his eyes, but there was also a question behind those cool blue eyeballs. I knew I had to tell him the truth. And so I did. I talked and talked and talked, telling Steve everything that my father had done to me, what I suspected he had done to my sisters and what had happened at the clubhouse. I have never seen a man so angry. Steve was so mad that I swear steam was coming out of his ears. I had heard that saying before, but thought that it was just an adage, but now I was almost a believer. Steve's face was redder than his father's red truck and his eyes were shooting lightning bolts at me. He began to swear that he was going back to my house and if he didn't kill my father that he would beat him until he couldn't move. I begged and pleaded for Steve to calm down. I told him that it was over, that it had been done and that nothing could undo it. I told him that if he killed my father or even if he beat him, the truth would come out and everybody in the city of Charlotte and all the area all around would hear about it. I told him that our classmates in school would hear.

Steve was emphatic. He didn't care who knew. I was his, I was his wife and he was going to make it right. Finally I convinced him that he couldn't make it right, it would never go away. I convinced him that it would not only hurt Shirley Jean and Patricia Ann, but it would hurt his own family when they found out he had married damaged goods. To his benefit, he said he didn't give a damn and anybody that didn't like it could just go to hell, his family or anyone else.

It took more than two hours to finally persuade Steve that the best thing for everybody was to put everything that had happened before this day behind us and to start life anew as of this moment. Finally he was agreeable, but told me that if he should meet my father anywhere in the world, even if it was in the middle of the church at high noon mass, there would be hell to pay. I understood that and said a prayer that God would not let these two meet. I knew if they did, one would likely die and the other one would wind up in jail.

It turned out that I could not have married a much finer man than Steve, but it also turned out that we had each made a bad decision. We had believed that our companionship was enough of a tie to last a lifetime. Unfortunately, that is not a good assumption.

Don't get me wrong. A companionship such as we had is more than sufficient for a lifetime, but a lifetime as friends, not as lovers and not as marriage partners. After we had been married about four and a half years, and after little Stevie—the most beautiful and most precious child in the world—had been conceived and had been born, Steve and I began to drift apart. Our goals began to separate and our aims became a little different. Being the kind of companions that we were, we frequently talked the situation over and made a friendly decision to go our separate ways. We didn't file for divorce right away; in fact we didn't even file for legal separation. We just decided to live apart and if either wanted a divorce at any time, than the other wouldn't object. We agreed that I would have custody of Stevie for most of the time, with Steve having equal rights for

Stevie to spend time with him as they both decided. That situation worked out quite well, and after some five or six years, Steve called to tell me he had finally met someone that 'lit his fire.' Surprisingly, he wanted to bring her out to my place to meet me and Stevie. I was agreeable and when Jennie and Steve got to my house, I was delighted to find that Steve had indeed chosen wisely, and to this day, Jennie and Steve are two of my closest friends, and I would like to believe that I am one of theirs.

As for me, I haven't really found anybody that 'lights my fire', although I have had several short affairs and will likely have more. In fact, I have my eyes on one of my co-workers at the webpage design firm, Chris, who is both cute and agreeable. I think we may get it together sometime soon, but to tell the truth, I am enjoying the liberty of playing the field. In this manner, it is my choice, not someone else's and I'm not forced to do anything that I don't want to do.

I won't lie and tell you that I find great pleasure in the sexual act because I don't, the memories are still too strong. But I will tell you that it is nice and sometimes even pleasant to be held close and loved by a kind and gentle man, but so far nothing has been extremely hot. Still, I have my hopes and my expectations, and I intend to keep on keeping on.

God, life is great. Sometimes.

Oh, as far as our father and our mother, I'll leave up to Patty to tell you all about that.

Patricia Ann

My two sisters make me sick. As I sit here listening to them make lame excuses for the deranged individual who was our father I could just puke. He was just a diabolical, deranged, depraved perverted child molester and that's about all there is to it. I don't care what kind of injury he suffered in the war, nor do I give a damn about his supposed Post-traumatic Stress Disorder. That didn't give him the right to abuse three children, much less his own children. We were the ones he was supposed to protect and you see what happened. I would bet money that it is likely that he did the same thing when he was over there. In fact, he was just like all men, just trying to get into the pants of all the girls that they can, and age or relations don't matter at all. They will screw anything that walks and might even get those who can't walk or don't know enough to run. Even a snake if it would just lay still.

The shrinks call them pedophiles, and that's just a convenient term to mask the true evil that they do. Men are all just naturally molesters and always have been and always will be, and that's the truth, the whole truth. Deep down, they don't respect us and they believe that we are their footstools. Hah.

Soft words and excuses like those that are being spouted by my sisters and supposedly 'learned' professionals are just a load of bull manure. I have heard of many veterans who have come home from war with head injuries and mental problems. There have been a lot of them from as long ago as World War Two in the middle of the 20th century. Many of those veterans took to drugs or alcohol. A lot of killed themselves or killed or hurt other people. Violence seems to have been a commonplace occurrence . But not child rape. Not molesting their own children. That is bestial. Those perverts didn't just all of a sudden become sexual predators, and there is just no excuse for it. I don't give a damn what some stupid shrink says, man's basic character is unchangeable and unchanging. Whatever was wrong with the creature that was our father would have been wrong for all his life. It didn't just suddenly come on and it didn't just suddenly disappear. That's just b.s. He knew what he was doing when he was doing it and he kept on doing it. In fact, if he were here today, he would be doing it again to some little girl somewhere. Thank God that he can't do it anymore.

And Shirley Jean... what the hell? She is just waiting for Mr. Right to come along. And what are you going to do, dear sister, when he does come along? You are going to marry him and breed his children—uh oh! Forgot. You can't breed, so I guess you will just have to adopt. But be careful, if you adopt a baby girl, he just might get to her the way our father and his 'friends' got to us. Better to adopt a boy baby. But don't feel too safe, he may be one 'those'... the ones who prefer boys. Best thing is not to adopt anyone. Even better, it is best not to get married. Or even better than that, tell Mr. Right just to keep on traveling. Wait for Ms. Right. That is the best of all. She certainly won't rape a baby girl... or if she does, it won't hurt. And she doesn't like boys, so a boy child isn't in danger.

Of course, if you live that sort of lifestyle, the kind that I live, you will have the stigma. Bull dyke, butch, Lezbo, etc, etc, etc. But names can't hurt, not like a deranged father or a 'friend' who has bought sexual favors from the kids. No, better to stay away from men altogether. My advice. Free for the taking.

Sure, like my two sisters, I was raped by my father. It started when I was five and continued until I left home at seventeen. He had learned that giving us girls pot and narcotics or even alcohol would let him do about anything he wanted to do. What he didn't realize was that after the first time, my organs were numb and stayed that way for more than twelve years. After the first time—which was just as painful as my sisters have said—I didn't feel anything. No pleasure, no pain, no sense of penetration. Evidently he didn't know it nor did his so-called friends. They could do it one after the other until they ran out of energy and it wouldn't make any difference to me. And they did do it, over and over and over. Sometimes as many as ten men in one night. Most of the time, my father had given me something that would make me feel good, believing that it would help me relax. But since I didn't feel anything anyway, I was about as relaxed as I could be. If they wanted to poke around in me, that was okay, just let me know when you finish.

The only thing I regret about the entire situation is that it took me three or four years to get over that feeling and the careful attention of my loving female friend before I could develop any sensation at all. Now, thank God, that time has passed and I can enjoy Candy's ministrations. That is what I have advised my two sisters to do, but they are too prudish. Guess our father ruined them forever. May he rot in hell.

Want to know what happened to him? Turns out that stuff he was drinking finally got to him. He developed cancer of the pancreas as well as cancer of the liver. They couldn't operate as it had advanced too far and the waiting list for transplants was so long and he was so far down the list that there was just no chance. Near the end they put him into an isolated chamber where they could keep him sedated, but the pain of the cancer eating into his pancreas and his kidney was so severe that it overrode the opiates that they would give him. Anyone standing outside his unit could hear him screaming in pain and it kept on eating away. The medical people did him a disservice by keeping him alive as long as possible, hoping to find a cure, but there was actually no hope. Finally, he just lapsed into unconsciousness and never came out of it. His final days were pure hell with unimaginable pain. I bet it was equal to the pain he inflicted on his three little girls. Good. Want to know how I knew he suffered? One of the nurses giving him his pain medicine was my good friend Candy. Did I forget to mention that she is a Registered Nurse? Do you think that perhaps she, knowing the true situation, may have adjusted his pain medicine just a small bit?

As for our mother, that is a horse of a different color. Or maybe I should say a whore of a different color. Turns out that the nightclub where our mother was working was a house of prostitution. When a man—or a woman—wanted a little sexual activity, he or she would inform the hostess—in this case, our mother—and she would make arrangements for a sex partner to be available. There was a charge, of course, and our mother would collect the fee and turn it in to the owner of the club. The owner of the club, a black woman from California, would pay my mother a percentage of the fee, pay the sex partner a share and then keep the rest for herself. The nightclub was a popular place, but didn't make a lot of money as a nightclub. But with low-price drinks, a dance floor, and willing and attractive sex partners, the place made a pretty good profit.

Our father had known what was going on and knew that sometimes our mother was the willing sex partner herself. He didn't give a damn, as long as she brought her earnings home to him. If she didn't make enough, then he would beat her with his belt, never hitting her face so that she could appear in public without anyone knowing our father was also a woman beater.

Part of me would like to believe what our mother told us about how our father was before the war and his head injury.

The rest of me just believes that was just a blow job she gave herself.

While our father was in the institution dying, the police raided the nightclub where my mother worked. Turns out that one of the customers was a female undercover cop and two of the 'willing' sex partners were not actually willing, but strung out on heroin and kept virtually captive and used over and over. The judge gave my mother twenty years in the federal pen as it turns out she was the one to give the heroin drug to the sex partners, and dealing in drugs was a lot more serious than simple prostitution. She was in prison while our father was dying and according to the guards, she didn't even ask how he was doing. When he finally died and they told her about his death, her only comment was, "Well, that's life."

So there you have it, the story of us three sisters. All so young, all so innocent. Now, one is hunting for Mr. Right to erase all of the bad memories. Sure. One is fairly well adjusted and seems to have come to grips with herself and who is determined to enjoy life, taking it as it comes. And one who has found that the fair sex is actually the better sex and that sex with the fair sex is the better sex. Did you get that?

As to what tomorrow may bring – the future is not ours to see.

'Bye.

www.ingramcontent.com/pod-product-compliance
Lightning Source LLC
Chambersburg PA
CBHW061447040426
42450CB00007B/1259